Pansies

Carol Barrett

For Michael,
With admiration
and gratitude ~
Carol
January 2019

SONDER
PRESS

Sonder Press
New York
www.thesonderpress.com

ISBN 978-0-9997501-3-1

First U.S. edition 2018
Printed in the USA
Distribution via Ingram

Author photo by Sarah Sargent

Acknowledgments

Artist Trust, a Washington state arts organization, provided a GAP grant in support of this work. Union Institute & University also provided a faculty research grant for the project.

The following publications contributed background information for vignettes in this collection:

The Reflector (Battle Ground, WA): "Census" (obituary, February 5, 1997, p. B-9)

The Columbian (Vancouver, WA): "Formula" ("Boy, 3, Cares For Baby After His Mother Dies" by Randall Black, February 18, 1996)

Italicized segments in "Cattails" are derived from Augusta R. Goldin's *Ducks Don't Get Wet* (New York: Crowell, 1965.)

This collection is offered with profound affection for the woman I call Abigail, for her family, and for mine.

For Sarah

Pansies

Contents

Pansies

PLAIN FOLKS LIVE IN my town. Even our food is plain: corn-on-the-cob, drumsticks, biscuits with jam. Apostolics cotton to what is plain. The plain truth is that God rewards the faithful with a bumper crop, blond and blue-eyed, rosy-cheeked. They border a man's table like pansies. After supper, those who have come of age go outside for a smoke.

Pansies are a persistent breed. They take to the same soil, year after year. You rarely find an aberration, a cast-off, a hybrid wild with defiance. They never crowd each other for the light. When night comes, those velvet hearts prepare to propagate.

Monet

WANTED: SECOND MOM FOR two-year-old girl whose mother works at home. Weekdays, flexible hours. Experience and references required. Must drive to location behind Anderson Dairy.

Thirty women called, one man. Most thought Sarah ideal for their place. Over half had infants. Where were the dimpled grandmothers who could use a little extra cash and company?

Sarah's Dad claimed veto power. He ruled out the man, the woman who thought mixing cement qualified as experience, and the one who lost everything in a mudslide two weeks earlier, certain that misfortune would rub off on Sarah. My problem is I want to say yes, yes; I'm a sucker for Girl Scout cookies or peanut brittle at the door.

Once I bought twenty miniature paintings from an old man at an art show in Wichita. Everybody passed him by – I couldn't stand it. *What's the story?* My friends asked, unwrapping those original holiday oils, one-inch square. His hands were all veins, patient with waterfalls and bridges, moss-covered barns and peach sunsets. Gone now, got to be. Years later, Sarah asks *Was that old man Monet?* I should have bought him out.

Interview

ON THE PHONE, ABIGAIL said right off she was fifteen, did I want someone older. I withheld judgment, intending a fair hearing. Now she sits at the edge of our couch, sparrow-like, listening to the questions scribbled in my notebook.

We begin with experience. Brothers and sisters fill a page. Sarah toddles over. *She's so cute.* School: *They found out I had asthma when I was twelve. I missed a lot, so I didn't go back.* I am ready to give this one up, resurrect her education. But no, she is working on a G.E.D. As for hobbies, she likes to make things. *Anything.* Her aspiration: *Maybe have a day care, I mean when I'm old enough.* Food brings a quick answer: *I don't eat much.*

Then I ask about spiritual values, presupposing no doctrine or practice. I simply want my child raised up in kindness. Stunned, she breathes out *Nothing is more important than God.* Apparently this should be obvious, like air. As for pay: *Whatever you want, it don't matter.* She won't budge. My final question, whether she smokes: *Not any more. Because of the asthma. I had to quit.*

I take a deep breath, for both of us.

Census

ALL DAY LONG THEY have been sawing boards for the new gymnasium. The smell of sawdust lingers for miles: it is the smell of newness, the old grain giving up its proud reign for the young ones just coming on. Abigail lets down her hair to shake it out, hands me the weekly *Reflector*. We have inched into the forest another twenty-five percent, and Chester Olin, eighty-three, is gone.

Welder, carpenter, Chester liked filing saws. Those many-splendored blades will be split among his sons: Jim and Ron, Dan and Dave, Virgil, Richard, Larry. Daughters assemble egg salad sandwiches in the church basement – Joyce and Judy, Jean and Mary. His first love, Orpha, passed from these woods in '38, bless her soul. Then Viola, his second, '89, bless her heart. But the rest will come: sixty-three grandchildren, ninety-three great grandchildren. He looks to have been a kind man. They'll fix him up, polish those rows of wavy hair till they gleam like saw teeth.

Bearing

I HESITATE TO PUT Abigail to work in the yard, but she says she doesn't mind, she helps her mother with the gardening too. I haven't met her mother yet. She's expecting her twelfth, must be strong. I picture her always indoors. But Abigail says she grows flowers and raises tomatoes, all kinds, to lengthen the season. She cans them for sauce.

As I turn clods Abigail pulls weeds, Sarah yanking the tops off dandelions, spreading their butter in little piles on the lawn. We heap compost into the wheelbarrow, fill in the low spots that puddle in the rain, Sarah riding the rim. In the sand pile, Abigail builds a child-size princess chair, complete with arms and head rest. Sarah sits on her damp throne, grinning.

Amazing, what the earth will bear.

The Dive

ALTERNATE EVENINGS I STRETCH out in the town pool, reserved for women who pay their small dues, eight to twelve disciples splashing away the strains of the day. Most are Apostolic, and conversation gets frothy fast. They chuckle at my progeny — only one child, past bearing. Marcia, two years my junior, lists fourteen grandchildren, and counting. For family reunions she rents the school gymnasium. One hundred forty-six ate casseroles last year.

The expectant mother consults her midwife in the fifth month, a host of stories from sisters, mothers, aunts. Ellen is the most beautiful woman I have ever seen. Eight months along, elegant as a marble Madonna, a sun-ripened pear. The baby bulges beneath her breasts, her long hair floating like a shawl of gold thread in the rippled tide. I imagine her Helen of Troy, the cause of envy, and war. Carrying her ninth, she climbs the blue stairs, navigates to the deep end. The two of them flip in a graceful backward arc. Breasts cushion the womb's perfect plunge. After the birth, she will bring her three-year-old to watch over this baby swaddled in its carrier at the water's edge.

Tomato Soup

I BEGIN ASKING ABIGAIL to make lunch. This is before we call her Abbie, a name familiar as coats in the hall closet, before her number has the ring of a nursery rhyme, a song that stays with me like a happy scent – my grandmother's roses, stocks of dill, or the pine needles my father always pronounced were fir, ignorance of natural identity an error equivalent to bad manners.

When I first put out a can of soup, Abigail fumbles, finally admitting she doesn't know how to do it. I try to hide the shock. *A can of soup?* True, I was a lousy cook at her age. But I had sisters mentored in the ways of cinnamon and asparagus. My ambitions were other.

It took me some time to figure out how this girl-child could escape such a simple task: Abigail only makes soup from scratch.

Chalk

ABIGAIL HAS A STREAK of artistic genius running through her hands. I return with groceries and find the most ornate drawings on Sarah's chalk board, mounted a few inches off the floor at the end of the hall. I never erase them. When I commend her skill, she avoids the chalk box for weeks.

One day, when Sarah complains she doesn't get mail like big folks, Abbie makes a miniature mailbox from an empty Kleenex carton, and the two of them fold scaled-down cards into envelopes with stamp replicas in the corner. When the cat chews up the children who ride the teeter totter in one of Sarah's storybooks, Abbie fits replacements that move up and down on the page, the stripes on their shirts shifting believably in the breeze. She makes elaborate fruit bowls out of play dough, teaches Sarah how to roll the grapes, crimp the lettuce for bite-size hamburgers. On the shelf in Sarah's bedroom yawns an exquisite clay baby with leather drum and headdress. Two inches high. I have learned not to say anything. Our small gallery is flourishing.

Rocking Song

ABIGAIL IS NOT ALLOWED to make music, and poetry is so close to song. One sleepy afternoon I suggest a lullaby, unaware I am calling in the devil. She wraps my baby girl double in a blue afghan and rocks her without melody, forward squeak echoing backward tilt, the clock in counterpoint, rain like a patio piano. I sit down to work. A little later Abbie tiptoes past my study, lays her bundle down in bed.

Now when Sarah's sleepy, she wants that same blue blanket, wants to be doubled close to the heart. She asks for stories. Sometimes, I sing them.

News

TODAY ABIGAIL CANNOT STOP talking. A house in Michigan burned down, children under their beds. No one would have known except a man was walking his dog and saw smoke. They pulled the kids out, limp as dishrags, but most still breathing. The smoke is still firing her story, cheeks flushed from the blaze: *No furniture or nothing. No insurance.* She goes over what must be done, as a block barn and stable rise up from our living room floor: bread and potatoes, school books, winter coats, a team of help when the ground is soft.

I think *this must be family,* this grief so engaged and specific. But I'm wrong, again. She doesn't know them. Her mom was talking on the phone to someone in Michigan. So the news comes: the names of the children, mitten and boot sizes. She is figuring what she can send.

At 6 o'clock the TV rolls through its blurring litany, off limits to Abbie and her kind. There is no burning house in Michigan. No man on a country road, dog or no dog. My news is the usual rotation of rape, murder, burglary, fraud. Street talk, trying to bring things home. *Human interest.*

Abbie does not see the world as I do. The tragedies in her life are ones she can do something about.

Fwa Fwa Doah

AFTER SUPPER ONE EVENING my little girl wants dessert. *Sorry honey. If we had some cookies, but we're all out.* Sarah answers *Fwa Fwa Doah*, matter-of-factly. Her Daddy and I are perplexed, this is a new one. *Fwa Fwa Doah*, more vigorous now. We begin a quiz. Is it something you eat? I ask. *No.* Where is it? She points to the living room, but the puzzle persists. Her father carries her there. Still pointing, out the window now. *Fwa Fwa Doah.* I can't make it out. Would Abbie?

I try to listen as if I'm Abbie, as if I understand her better than her own mother. Ah – it's the car Sarah's pointing to. The car? I say. Sarah nods. I think for a moment. You want to go somewhere? Nods again. I think *Oreo, vanilla wafer.* Finally, *Fwa Fwa Doah*: Safeway Store.

Formula

I GET TEASED FOR being over-protective. When I took Sarah at six months in her bunting and hood to see my sister in the hospital, I got *Where's the snow storm?* Some cold you can prepare for; some you can't. Among Apostolics there's always an emergency plan: look out for the next one in line.

Tray Hubbard turns three in April. When his mother fell asleep and didn't wake up, he fixed Cheerios for Kiana, a year and a half, stuffed toilet paper rolls in her diapers to keep her dry. I hear this story first from Abbie — *those poor kids* — later it's in the paper. When he heard knocking at the door, Tray moved a chair, climbed up and undid the lock. Authorities estimate his mother had been dead two days.

Sarah will turn three in October. No one ahead of her, no one behind.

Meditation

WHEN SARAH IS SLEEPING, Abigail does up my dishes — an hour or more the way she works it, stacking everything in concentric assembly on the counter, drawing scalding water, no dish to impair the flow, handling each piece like a bead on a rosary, rinsing bowls as if they were little sailboats. Finally, the drying rack, a thick towel, cupboards replenished with their shining stock. With Abigail there is never any risk of nicking, unlike my sister, who managed to break two of the wine glasses we were given as wedding presents in a single meal — I stopped her midway through the chore.

Something more than prevention of catastrophe inspires Abbie's patience with my caked mayonnaise and egg yolk. Slipping down the hall I watch her back, the loving way she swirls the cloth, hands the silver to the steam. Even when I tell her she needn't be so careful, she does not speed up. Doing dishes is a meditation, silky thoughts stirring in the suds, everything coming out clean and sparkling again. A leaf drifts down outside the window. Another spoon at rest.

The Changing

ONE OF THE LAST days of summer, I take Sarah and two of her cousins to Yale Lake, out past Yacolt and Amboy, the Lewis River dammed up to a blue purpose, white floats marking the swimming hole. Weekday, few boats about, I sit in the pebbles, watch the girls. An Apostolic mother is stretched out nearby on a daisyed slope, talking with her teenage daughter plucking the grass, two coolers on hand. Eight more of her children in the lake, bobbing like iced watermelon. The mountain smiles down at us, close as a post card. A toddler stamping the shallows scrunches her face like a squirrel, clutches her fanny. She waddles over, any mom will do, says *pooped*. I guide her to the grass, where her mother leans on one elbow, calls for Rachel, perhaps nine, who slips from an innertube and plies her way across the stony bottom. She will make the change. School will start up in the morning, but the lessons began a long time ago.

Cupcakes

SARAH'S NEW PRESCHOOL TEACHER sends a note home: *If you want to bring cupcakes for your child's birthday, please sign up. If you don't celebrate birthdays in your home, we will honor that too.* I hadn't thought about this before: some kids never hear their name in that clamorous chorus, lick their fingers to snuff a smoking candle out.

Sad, somehow. Must be a good reason. I acknowledge the teacher's attention to difference. She's friendly right back, tells me to enjoy the sunshine. Wants to get home to plant some bulbs but she'll probably get caught behind the bus. It really slows her down. *You know those Apostolics. Thirteen kids at every stop.*

Dervish

SARAH LOVES TO TWIRL, skirts swirling like a contessa in the living room. Any melody can accompany these pirouettes, but the skirt must spin like the petals of a daisy turned on the stem. Applause is nothing next to such natural aires.

Abigail arrives one day with pink ballet slippers gleaned from a second-hand store in Yacolt. *Look Sarah, I brought you some dancin' shoes.* Small as an elf's, they fit like Cinderella's and she's all a'twirl. I marvel at this spiraling happiness, this unexpected footing. Abigail has never owned a pair, nor her sisters, nor anyone she knows. The body is divine. Dance is the body's seduction, unholy and beyond grace. Sarah is outside the fold. Abbie will not condemn her whirling dervish. Dancing on the outskirts of Abbie's culture, I've dipped my skirts in judgment more than once. These magic shoes make me want to take it all back.

It Don't Matter

THE AVERAGE AMERICAN SPENDS a third of life sleeping. The average English teacher spends that third on papers: mountains of text, rocky with errors. You would have to be a goat to get through them nimbly.

Abigail is doing splendidly. I tell her how pleased we are, decide to wait awhile to correct the one error that persists in her grammar. I don't want to be so critical, so soon. But I don't want Sarah too used to it, either.

Before long I'm enchanted, postpone, again, correcting those *It Don'ts*.

All these years my father has drummed in the difference between lay and lie. But I forget who is supposed to stretch out how. I have cats lying and people laying and I still don't get enough sleep. As for Abigail — she has won me over. I side with her, deciding *it don't matter*.

Omissions

ABBIE'S RIDE HOME IS late. On the way back from Costco for groceries, her folks' van pulls up. I invite them in, offering a bowl of homemade split pea soup. Jessica, current baby in the family, sits on her mother's lap, gumming some of the green goo. Her dad says how good it is, asks for my recipe. Onions! He exclaims. That's it. Delicious! A quick reflex from Abbie's Mom, his cook of twenty years: I thought you didn't like onions. Jessica is gurgling and blowing happy bubbles in my soup. Listen to you, I say, trying to cover an awkward moment. Are you going to be a poet too? Her mother laughs out loud, a laugh larger than the long absence of onions.

Courting

ZUCCHINI IS LEGION HERE, and cucumbers almost as prolific. One day over cucumber sandwiches, I tell Abbie the family story they always conjure up: the time star quarterback Skip Reeves asked my sister Kathy out and took her fishing. He brought the bait, she brought the lunch. After hours in the boat, no luck, he asked for some grub, ready for a roll of salami, a squirt of sharp mustard to stem the tide. Instead, she unwrapped a dainty cucumber sandwich, skin gored with a fork. Skip was mortified, but devotion won out. Abbie likes Kathy, and laughs. They sound alike when they laugh. It is a sound like a condiment, not the main dish.

Knowing proms and movies are out of the question, I ask Abbie what kids in her church do for dates. *Oh, we go camping* she says. I'm shocked, try to imagine *his* and *hers* tents. *Or we go to the beach* she adds casually. It's a three-hour drive! I was never permitted such a trip. *What do you do at the beach?* Blunt now, I admit. *Oh, we go swimming, or play volleyball.* Volleyball. I think about that. It begins to register: dating Apostolic style is a group venture. Who you ride with, that's the thing. Not whose rowboat, whose truck.

Buns

FORBIDDEN: TO CUT A woman's hair. Apostolic tresses flow long and blond as Rapunzel's. I have not learned the source of taboo. What need has God for hair?

Perhaps a man is stunned when his bride lowers her ropes onto his climbing desire. She binds him to fidelity. Perhaps survival depends on distinction: no tampering with fair locks, girls marked for the fold.

Bunhead: derogatory term for Apostolic. Designs on a woman's head abound. The hair is braided, knotted, rolled, tied and wound. Any twisted form, so long as the flax may be felled by a man's urgency. It will drape her breasts and buttocks. When it catches his mouth, he might taste gold. He might measure his wealth by the strands brushing the backs of his hands, by what they portend: little faces asleep in the next room.

One afternoon Abigail gathered Sarah's hair in a makeshift ponytail, then turned the filaments like a cinnamon bun, securing the coif with a final band and tuck. We admired her bun. Sarah looked like a dancer, studied herself in the mirror. Later, hair washed, she told me: *Mommy, I want the hamburger hair-do.*

The Gift

ABBIE IS BEAMING. SHE is getting married. *Congratulations* I say, unable to swallow, our blessed angel lost to some earthly creature I have never met. I bring myself to ask his name. *Rick?* I ask again. Even his name is dull.

It is a puzzle what to give her. I meander the shops, trying to imagine a bright future, resort to something I would have liked myself: a quartet of crystal dessert plates, heart-shaped. Already I taste pralines and cream, thinking *any girl would go for them.* She is only sixteen. Somehow, that raises the odds.

Several weeks after the wedding, Abbie invites me by to see her gifts, perhaps because I have asked. They are still stacked in the spare bedroom. She is proudest of the box from Rick's folks, opens the set. *I just love them she says,* ring finger encircling the rim.

They remind me of a cafeteria in Texas I used to haunt: plain ceramic, single dark green band. Plain as daylight.

Wedding Suite

Church

WE FIND IT AT the end of a dirt road, without benefit of sign or steeple. The pews are teeming with mussed cotton dresses and squirming boys. My dark, clipped hair a double novelty: I remember walking up to the tank at Lewisville Fish Hatchery in a red sweater, how many eyes swarmed to the surface. Here, no familiar edifice: no piano, pulpit, altar, cross. Sarah is overdressed in her Daisy Kingdom petticoats, which poof on the bench like a parasol. The women have topped their heads with handkerchiefs, the men clad in short-sleeved plaid shirts, the kind I expect at Bingo games. Everyone is talking.

Wedding Party

ABIGAIL LOOKS LOVELY, WHITE cotton dress, one row of lace, scarf gracing the bun her sister did up for her, a few more strands wafting at the neck than usual. She carries no flowers. Rick has rented a black tux with no tie. Apostolics do not wear ties. They are a sign of the world.

There is no pastor. The man down front is the deacon on call this week. A short fellow, he stutters at the beloved. Abigail's father is everywhere, humming like a washing machine. Her mother is nowhere to be seen. Getting out of the van with Abigail's dress and the sandwiches for the reception, she has closed the door on her youngest child's arm and is over at urgent care getting it cast.

Ceremony

ABIGAIL AND RICK WALK down the center aisle, claimed and together. There is no music. Rick's head is turned somewhere to the rafters, exactly the way my husband's was. The deacon marries them. I cannot hear what is being said. They kneel and I presume they are blessed. We bend to prayer, but catch no kiss, the lines of a wedding chant passed through a dozen ideas of melody. The couple recedes. I smile as Abigail passes. She tucks her chin, biting her lip. It is done.

Reception

THE TUNA AND EGG salad sandwiches are good. A dozen of Abigail's sisters and friends serve them up in the church basement. Rick's eyes are still in the corners of things. Long tables crowd the room, each with a mayonnaise jar full of wild daisies. Only the center table has a cloth. This is where Abbie's family groups. She invites us to sit here, but there is no room. Outside every door, teenagers chum up, giggling and smoking. Thus my Abbie girl is married. I cannot think of anything else for days.

Walls

AN APOSTOLIC MOM WANTS Abbie for three little girls the same days she's here with Sarah. *Can Sarah come too?* I better check this out.

Shoes form a prim row at the door. The house has simple lines, oak floor. The girls' mom is making bread, shows me the place, closing the bedroom door. All the girls are wearing dresses. The oldest is four, has a cold. Toys, books, dolls. A pasture of cows. No traffic. Sarah has spotted the tricycles. I decide it's a go.

When I relay the excursion to Sarah's dad, I realize *the walls were bare.* In a rush, it comes to me what Abbie was saying about her wedding. I asked if a relative would handle photography. *No* she said, *we don't take pictures.* I thought I understood. *I didn't want a video of our wedding either* I told her. I wanted to remember it my way.

But I hadn't understood. *We don't take pictures.* She meant the walls, not the wedding.

Cattails

ABIGAIL TAKES SARAH THREE blocks over to the library, and they return with an armload of books. How does she find such things? My jaunts there produce the most mundane woods: paper leaves, a baby squirrel with fake fur you can rub. At home, Sarah has real squirrels to watch. They drink from the bird bath. But Abbie's tours take her someplace else, to the coves where ducks preen. *Ducks don't get wet. Oil and water do not mix.* Her voice pecks through the pages: *Pintail ducks and mallards search for pondgrass and wild rice. Blue-winged teals dip for mussels, clams, crayfish and crabs. Wood ducks eat duckweeds and grass seeds, wild celery and lily. Shoveler ducks scoop up water and strain it for snails, tadpoles and shrimps.* Sarah listens to the litany: harlequin, canvasback, eider duck, scoup. She watches these new words fly in our sky, explains how the raindrops roll right off their backs.

This afternoon, she and Abbie have gathered a handful of bluejay feathers from under the hemlock. They dip them in a bowl of salad oil, float them in the bath, two girls learning the natural ways of the world, voices blending like cattails in the wind. Tomorrow falls away, oil on water. High above, the ducks are flying home.

A Week of Wife

DURING DAYLIGHT RICK SCALES the walls of the world, roofer with his father's firm. He sees a lot from up there, hoisting tiles, tar, nails and tools. Home at dark. Abigail keeps supper waiting, her days long and lonesome. On weekends she takes the laundry to her mother's house, plays volleyball with the younger kids, is fed and sent home for another week of wife.

I remember summers as a camp counselor on Silver Lake, Abbie's age. One day off each week, we took the laundry home for a hot shower, ham and pea casserole. How good the other girls looked when they got back, clean and fed, the imprint of a mother's hand on their jeans. We scuttled between hard duty and restoration, veterans of campfire smoke, teaching the names of ferns, pressing them in see-through placemats – bracken, sword, licorice, maidenhair, woods – giving all we could. Most of our campers cried on the bus home.

Showing

THE COLOR OF STRAW, Abigail's favorite sweater floats shapeless, huge sleeves pushed to the elbows for dishes at the sink. More and more she arrives in this sagging blanket, her body disappearing inside. Years before, I wore a mammoth mauve sweater my mother despised, pockets drooped to my knees. I could shrink in its warm folds, walk the beach in the fog. Nobody knew me.

One day, barely in the door, Abbie tells me she's pregnant. Amid soft exclamations, the calling back of Sarah's conception, I glance instinctively at the sweater's mid-section. Impossible to tell. I wonder when she'll tip one hundred. Abigail and baby pass the weeks hidden in that soft, ambiguous cloak. Everything is changing, for her, for us. This life on the brink, the imperative of fruitfulness. And you can't even tell.

Going Hawaiian

I FIGURE ABBIE WILL be gone for good when her baby comes. Not quite. A little bored with just one, she's taken on three more, Hawaiian girls, invites Sarah to join them on Fridays. Sarah jumps like a pogo stick. She would go anywhere with Abbie. And she gets to hold the baby.

Kika, Kelii, Kaui – I can't keep them straight. Sarah has no trouble. They say learning another language so young is easy as pie. *Poi.* Sarah tells me the snacks are different in Hawaii. *Oh?* I ask. *Yes Mommy. They eat spaghettios, it's kind of spicy.*

Barbie II

I VOWED NEVER TO have a Barbie doll in the house, but Sarah gets one for her birthday. I'm stuck. Can this culture of fashion be crossed? For Christmas I launch a career kit, making models of what Sarah wants to be when she grows up. Barbie gets a pilot suit with gold buttons and a blue flight bag, pink veterinarian scrubs with dogs and cats on the pockets. *They're so cute* even Abigail says. Sarah's cousins all want duplicates. We haul out the boxes of scraps, beads and baubles gleaned from garage sales, and the project takes off. Sarah wants a construction worker now, a forest ranger with binoculars. Abigail knows the bazaar circuit, suggests a display at *Once Upon A Child*. We scour Goodwill stores for discards. Stacks of naked dolls clog the bathroom, where Sarah shampoos their hair and works the thick tangles out with cream rinse. I float the enterprise at my mother's church, near canisters of divinity and cone wreaths.

Somewhere on a country road a new image is forming: Barbie has removed her eye shadow and earrings, her long blond hair braided neatly down the center of her back. She dons a plain cotton dress and simple scarf. The box reads "The Bride."

Ten

THIS MORNING I MEET Helen of Troy in the pharmacy. Sarah has bronchitis, and we've come for cherry-flavored Amoxicillin, chewable. Her kids have had the stuff too. I remind her of the dive with her ninth – she will always be diving in my mind. But she doesn't remember, she has ten now. The baby's in the car with one of the kids. Another's got her hand, and one in the stroller. She comments how Sarah has grown, as if she were my aunt or my cousin, as if one child were equal in her mind, this moment, to ten.

Pensée

ABBIE AND HER MOTHER are both pregnant. I hold this revelation like a glass ball that rains snow when turned upside down. Two women, friends, side by side, fertile mounds, Saturn with her rings. They are Mary and Elizabeth. They are mother and child, *with child, with child.*

Sorting seed in the garden, I recall other names for pansies: heartsease, jump-up-and-kiss, love-in-idleness. Nothing idle here. The French call it *pensée,* meaning thought. My grandmother put in a purple clump near the border of her land. I slip a light trowel under these smiling descendants of violets, move them to the front porch. They will multiply like thoughts. They will nod in the breeze, cheer my comings and my goings, little faces turned to the light.

Author Note

Carol Barrett holds doctorates in both clinical psychology and creative writing. She coordinates the Creative Writing Certificate Program at Union Institute & University. She also teaches in the Creativity Studies Program at Saybrook University. Carol has published in psychology, religious studies, gerontology, women's studies, medical, education, and dance and art therapy journals, in addition to literary magazines and anthologies. Her collection *Calling in the Bones* won the Snyder Prize from Ashland Poetry Press. She has received awards from the National Endowment for the Arts, the National Institute of Mental Health, and the National Science Foundation.

The present work came about when Carol hired a babysitter who was an Apostolic Lutheran — a group of largely Finnish descent, about whom there is currently no book in English. The group forbids the practice of birth control in any form. The bond that was forged between Carol's daughter and her Apostolic babysitter, called "Abigail" in this collection of true stories, is the center of the work. Along the way, Carol was challenged to transcend her initial impressions and prejudices about the community and its values.